ESTHER

Queen for a Reason

Susan Martins Miller

Illustrated by
Al Bohl

ISBN 1-58660-943-2

Published by Barbour Publishing, Inc., P.O. Box 719, Uhrichsville,
Ohio 44683, www.barbourbooks.com

 Member of the
Evangelical Christian
Publishers Association

Printed in the United States of America.
5 4 3 2 1

ESTHER

LIFE IN THE CITY OF SUSA

1

Esther Is Taken

The lively children giggled and chased each other down the road, while the women talked quietly among themselves. Occasionally a mother would raise her voice slightly or give a stern look to a child who was wandering too far away or getting too loud. This was an ordinary part of the day—drawing water from the well late in the afternoon and walking back to a row of modest houses where the Jews lived in the city of Susa.

Esther walked with the women now, although most of them were older than she was. She did not often have much to contribute to their conversation, which was usually about husbands and children. She did not truly fit in, but somehow she did not fit in with the energetic, squealing children either. She had grown past that stage. She was not a child, but she was not quite a woman.

As the group turned the last corner of the dusty road leading home, Esther's heart began to pound, and she could hear the gasps of the women around her. Soldiers were leaving their street! This could mean only one thing: Once again they had come to take a beautiful young woman to become part of the king's harem. Esther ran as fast as she could. Water sloshed out of the heavy jug in her arms. When she reached

FEAR FILLS ESTHER'S HEART.

her own house, she threw open the wooden door and began to shout.

"Cousin! Cousin!" Esther hurried from room to room looking for her cousin Mordecai, who had taken her in when she was orphaned and raised her as his own daughter. "Cousin Mordecai, where are you?"

She found him sitting silently in his room. "Esther, darling," he said, "come sit with me."

Esther stood still and demanded the truth. "They've taken someone again, haven't they?" Esther's voice shook with fear. "Tell me who, Cousin. Who was it?"

Mordecai was very slow to answer. At last he said in a hushed whisper, "Rebekah."

Esther put her hand to her mouth to stop the scream which welled up inside her. "Rebekah? My friend Rebekah? But, Cousin, Rebekah is no older than I am."

"THEY TOOK REBEKAH."

"WILL THEY COME FOR ME?"

Mordecai reached out and pulled Esther down on the bench beside him. She laid her head on his shoulder as he stroked her hair.

"Esther, you are very beautiful."

"Oh, Cousin, you have been telling me that all my life. You just say that because you love me."

"No, Esther, this time I say it as a warning. It has been almost a year now since King Xerxes began his search for a new queen. And you have changed so much during this year. You no longer look like a child. You are becoming a woman, and you are very beautiful."

Esther sat up straight and looked at her cousin's worried face. "You think they will come for me, don't you, Cousin?"

"Yes, Esther, I do."

The girl stood up and stomped her foot. "But, Cousin, how many women does the king need to choose from? The soldiers have already rounded up hundreds from among the Persians and Jews. Surely one of them has pleased the king."

Mordecai shook his head sadly. "I cannot explain it, Esther. And I pray that it will not happen to you." He paused and brightened his face. "Come, my child, let us have our meal."

Reluctantly, Esther took the hand her cousin offered, and they went together to the small room where they prepared their food together each evening. Mordecai tried several times to begin a conversation about a more pleasant subject, but Esther did not respond. She felt such an odd mixture of feelings: anger at the king's cruel method of choosing a new queen; grief for her friend Rebekah; fear that she, too, would be taken from her home and forced into a strange life. For years she had been yearning to grow up and take her place in the adult world; now she wished she could remain a child—at least until the king chose his new queen.

Esther went about her daily tasks as usual for the next several days. She cleaned the house, kept the water jug full, and made sure her cousin had good food to eat each evening. She loved to go to the marketplace and choose the vegetables and argue with the merchants about a fair price. Some of them pretended to hide when they saw her coming with her basket slung over her arm. This was a game they had been playing with Esther since she was a small girl and had come with her cousin to the market each day. Now she came alone, and the playful bartering still made it fun.

"Joseph, I want only the best vegetables you have today," she said, as she said every day.

"Then you will have to pay the best price," he answered. Esther's favorite merchant placed a tray of fresh vegetables in front of her and watched as she began her selection.

"YOU MUST HIDE!"

"This one is too soft; I will not pay full price," she said authoritatively. "And this one is too small; you picked it too soon."

"Very well. I will sell those to someone who is not such an expert as you are." Joseph smiled at Esther. Then something behind him caught his eye, and his smile faded quickly. He spoke urgently. "Esther, you must hide! Right now!"

It was too late. Before Esther could respond to Joseph's warning, her elbow was grabbed roughly, and she was spun around to look straight into the eyes of a soldier. Her basket was knocked to the ground. Quickly she looked around. There were several other soldiers nearby, their swords ready. No one could risk helping her.

"Cousin!" she screamed. "Find my cousin!" Joseph had already run off toward the business district where Mordecai worked, close to the king's palace. As she was dragged along, Esther

15

looked frantically through the crowd, searching for her cousin's full dark beard and distinctive, wide-set eyes. She was afraid she would be taken to the palace and never allowed to see her cousin again.

Suddenly Mordecai burst through the crowd and blocked the way of the soldiers. "Let her go," he demanded. "She's only a child." Esther clutched for her cousin's arm and held on tightly.

"Perhaps she is a child in your eyes," the soldier responded, "but she will be prepared to meet the king as a woman. Her beauty is obvious even now, and with the right adornment, she will be very lovely." He began to push her forward again. Esther tightened her grip on Mordecai's arm, and he moved quickly to keep up with the long strides of the soldier. Familiar faces flew past them—neighbors, friends, merchants—would she ever see these people again? Rebekah's

"LET HER GO!"

"COUSIN! COUSIN!"

mother was in the crowd, her face twisted in anguish. For a fleeting moment, Esther was comforted by the thought that she might see Rebekah again.

Abruptly, another soldier raised his arm to stop Mordecai's movement. When he resisted, her cousin was struck and knocked to the ground, stunned. The distance between them grew rapidly, and she knew he would never catch up.

"Cousin! Cousin!"

There was no answer.

2

THE NEW QUEEN

"Oh, Rebekah, your skin has such a lovely color," Esther said to her friend. "That new cream Hegai gave you is really working."

"Thank you, Esther," her friend answered. "Hegai is pleased with the results." She shrugged her shoulders. "But I don't really care. Why does it matter what my skin looks like?"

Esther sighed in agreement. "I know. We've

IN THE KING'S HAREM

been here for four years. We spend all our time making ourselves beautiful. The whole reason is to please the king and be chosen as his queen—and we don't want to be queen."

"All I want is to go home," Rebekah groaned. "They give us special food, expensive perfumes, beauty treatments, oil baths, maids to wait on us. And it's all for nothing. We'll never have husbands to appreciate our beauty. We'll always be a part of the king's harem, and he doesn't even know our names."

The conversation was interrupted by a gentle knock on Esther's door.

"Come in," she called.

One of her seven maids stepped into the room. "Your cousin is outside the palace, Esther."

"In the usual place?" Esther asked, moving toward the large window at the end of her room.

"Yes, ma'am."

"ALL I WANT IS TO GO HOME."

Esther carefully drew back the edge of the curtain and looked out. For many years, Mordecai had held an important job which allowed him to be near the palace. Hegai, the servant in charge of the young women waiting to be called by the king, had taken a special liking to Esther as soon as she had entered the palace. He had given her comfortable rooms in the best part of the palace and freedom to move about the courtyards if she wished. If she was careful, she could talk to Mordecai quite often.

Casually, Esther wrapped a light shawl around her slender shoulders and strolled down the hallway and out into the courtyard, bright with sunlight. Hegai would be alarmed if she exposed her flawless skin to direct sunlight, but he had agreed that fresh air would add color to her cheeks. She had long ago convinced him to allow her to take vigorous walks around the courtyard,

WAITING FOR MORDECAI'S VOICE

as long as she stayed out of the sun.

Esther walked once around the courtyard and then selected a low stone bench set close to the high palace wall and under a generous shade tree. She began to whistle a familiar melody from her girlhood. Soon she heard her cousin's voice.

"How are you, my dear cousin?" Mordecai's soft voice came clearly through a spot where the stones in the wall were not quite joined.

Esther smiled briefly and answered, "I am fine, Cousin. I am glad you came today. I only wish I could see your face instead of talking to you through this wall."

"And how is Rebekah? Her mother sends her love."

"She is very homesick, Cousin. She wants to go home. We all do. But tell her mother that Rebekah looks lovely and rested."

"You have not told them, have you, Esther?"

MORDECAI SPEAKING THROUGH THE WALL TO ESTHER

"That I am Jewish?" she answered. Mordecai asked this question every time they spoke together. "No, Cousin, I have not. But I still do not understand why it must be a secret. Surely they knew they were taking Jewish girls when they rounded us up."

"I cannot explain, Esther. I just have a feeling that things would not go well for you right now if they knew you were Jewish."

"Perhaps they would let me come home. Perhaps the king does not want a Jewish queen."

Mordecai did not answer right away. "Let's not argue. We don't have time for that."

Esther hid her frustration. "Yes, Cousin."

"I must go now. I will come again."

Esther sat on the bench for several minutes, looking around and wondering if anyone had seen her talking. Since Mordecai was out of sight, it would seem as if she were talking to herself, and

"MY TURN?"

that would surely lead to questions. Satisfied that she had not been seen, Esther got up and walked around the courtyard one more time.

When she returned to her room, Hegai was waiting for her.

"I've been looking all over for you, Esther," he said sternly.

Esther's heart began pounding. Perhaps someone had seen her after all. "I was in the courtyard, taking a walk. You have given your approval for that."

Hegai shook his head and waved his hand. "No, it's not that, Esther. I came to tell you it's your turn."

"My turn?" she questioned.

"Yes. Your turn to go to the king."

Now her heart felt as if it would stop beating. She had not thought this would ever really happen. "When?" she asked.

"WHAT ARE YOU GOING TO DO?"

"In three days," Hegai answered. "You may choose anything in the harem to take with you—your clothes, your perfumes, a gift for the king. Choose carefully, Esther. You are so very beautiful. Perhaps you will be the one to please the king."

Hegai left, and Esther stood motionless for a long time. After four years in the king's harem, even Esther had come to believe that she truly was a beautiful young woman. But was she beautiful enough to be chosen as queen? If she were chosen, would she be able to see Mordecai openly and often?

The door swung open, and Rebekah ran in breathlessly.

"I just heard! Oh, Esther, what are you going to do?"

"I. . .I. . .I'm not sure. I suppose I should ask Hegai's advice. He has been so kind to me."

ESTHER MEETING THE KING

The next three days were a flurry of activity for Esther and Hegai. Rebekah was always nearby, wanting to spend every moment possible with her friend. Esther trusted Hegai's advice and made her choices simply. The clothes she selected flattered her delicate frame and distinctive coloring. She would not pretend to be someone she was not; she was a simple girl with natural beauty, and this is what she presented to the king. When she was introduced to King Xerxes, she bowed deeply and followed meekly as she was led to his rooms.

The next morning, the palace buzzed with the news that King Xerxes was going to make a proclamation. Esther stood in the courtyard and gazed up at the balcony where the king would appear. The royal trumpeters stepped forward, raised their instruments, and announced the arrival of King Xerxes.

"I HAVE FOUND MY QUEEN!"

In a loud voice for all to hear, Xerxes said simply, "I have found my queen. There shall be a great royal banquet in honor of Queen Esther."

3

MORDECAI WARNS THE KING

Mordecai sat very still and held his breath, hardly able to believe that what he was hearing could be true. He had his back pressed to the wall outside the palace, afraid even to breathe. The conversation just around the corner reached his ears easily during a moment when not many people were nearby.

"Tonight at midnight," the hushed voice

MORDECAI OVERHEARS A PLOT.

said. "We will enter the palace at the end of our shift and wait for the moment to come."

Another voice answered in a harsh whisper. "The knife will be under my cloak. When dawn comes, the people will awaken and be glad that we have gotten rid of King Xerxes."

The voices trailed away, covered by the shuffling of feet. Cautiously, Mordecai let out his breath and stepped silently to the corner. Slowly, he looked around the edge of the wall at the backs of the two men walking away as their cloaks fluttered in the breeze. Even though they had whispered, Mordecai thought he had recognized the voices, and now he was sure who the men were. They had never caused trouble before; they simply stood guard at the palace gate day after day, making conversation with those who passed by. Even Mordecai had spoken to them quite frequently. And now these

MORDECAI RECOGNIZES THE EVIL MEN.

two soldiers were conspiring to kill the king. They stood guard under the authority of Haman, one of the king's highest officials. Mordecai had never liked Haman, even when they were young boys, but he could hardly believe that Haman would be involved in such an evil plot.

Mordecai found a bench and sat down trying to appear calm while he thought things through. What would Haman have to gain from trying to kill the king? Xerxes had already promoted him to a very high level. Perhaps Haman had nothing to do with it; perhaps the men were planning to overthrow Haman as well. If Xerxes were killed, what would happen to Esther? The longer Mordecai sat, more confusing questions flooded his mind and made it hard for him to think clearly.

Stroking his beard, Mordecai made up his mind. Esther had to be told. There was no way

SENDING A MESSAGE TO ESTHER

Xerxes would listen to someone like Mordecai, but Esther was the new queen, and she was the only one who could possibly get Xerxes to believe his life had been threatened.

Mordecai hurried around to the palace gate. Ever since Esther had been made queen, they had been able to see each other in the outer courtyard where Esther received many of her visitors. Although they were surrounded by many other people, it was better than whispering through a crack in the wall. As usual, he was admitted to the courtyard, and a servant was sent to inform Esther of his arrival.

As soon as she saw Mordecai, the beautiful queen knew something was terribly wrong.

"Cousin! What is it?" She clutched his arm in alarm. "Are you ill?"

"No, Esther, nothing like that. But your husband is in danger."

"My husband?" Esther was puzzled. What would make her cousin know about the king's business?

"I overheard some men talking today while I was working. I know who they are, Esther, and they mean business. It was Bigthana and Teresh, two of the officers who stand guard at the gate."

"What are you talking about, Cousin?"

"They want to kill the king! Tonight! At midnight. You must tell him, Esther, for your own sake. If something happens to Xerxes, do you really think they would have any use for you?"

The color drained from Esther's face as the truth of what Mordecai said sunk in. "All right," she said, "tell me what you heard."

Mordecai retold the whole conversation and explained what he knew about the officers he had seen and heard.

MORDECAI PACES AND WAITS FOR NEWS.

"I do not know if the king will believe me," Esther said at last. She knew Mordecai would not make up a plot like the one he described, but she was not sure the king would believe it. "But I will try to speak to him and tell him what you have said."

Mordecai paced back and forth outside the palace gate all day. When it was time for the midday meal, he hardly noticed. Instead, he kept walking. He forced himself to stroll casually and stop to talk to people every few minutes, trying not to appear concerned about anything unusual. Each time he passed Bigthana and Teresh standing at the gate, he nodded politely and acted as naturally as he could. As the hours wore on, he began to wonder if Esther would reach the king in time. It was now late in the afternoon. Soon it would be time for new guards to come stand at the gate during the night. Bigthana and Teresh

KEEPING WATCH ON THE EVIL GUARDS

would be difficult to follow. Mordecai would not be allowed inside the palace, but the guards would surely find a way past their fellow soldiers. Where was Esther? he wondered. What could possibly be keeping her so long?

The end of the day came, and Bigthana and Teresh turned over their duties to other guards. Just as Mordecai had feared, they withdrew into the protection of the palace itself. Before they were out of sight, Mordecai saw Teresh softly touch his side, as if checking on the weapon he planned to use that night. Mordecai could go only as far as the courtyard to wait for word from Esther. In just minutes, Bigthana and Teresh were inside the palace and out of sight. Unable to sit still, Mordecai continued his pacing, circling the courtyard over and over, faster and faster.

Suddenly, Haman barged into the courtyard

HAMAN SHOUTING AT MORDECAI

from inside the palace.

"Mordecai!" he shouted. "How dare you?"

"Did you know about this, Haman? Were these men acting on your orders?"

"I don't know what you are talking about," Haman said spitefully. Everyone could see his hatred for Mordecai. "Because of you, two of my finest officers are going to be hanged. According to the queen, it was you who accused the two guards of plotting to kill the king. How dare you get involved in matters which are none of your business?"

Mordecai answered quietly, "The well-being of the king is the business of every citizen."

"Why must you use every opportunity to stir up trouble?" Haman was red in the face and speaking very loudly.

Mordecai remained calm. "I simply did my duty. If the officers are guilty, that is their own fault. I am not responsible for the punishment they face." He turned to walk away.

"You must pay for this!" Haman shouted. "I am more powerful than you realize!"

Mordecai started to respond to Haman. But he stopped himself before he spoke. The important thing was that Esther was safe. There would be no point in arguing further with Haman. Feeling the eyes of the crowd on him, Mordecai forced himself to take steady, straight steps until he was once again on the street outside the palace.

4

HAMAN'S PLOT

"Can you believe that the king has promoted Haman again?" said Joseph to Mordecai one morning in the marketplace.

"Haman has been a very efficient officer," said Mordecai, trying to be kind. He had a lot of things on his mind, and he did not wish to stand in the street discussing Haman. He lifted his eyes to survey the vegetables.

SHOPPING AND HEARING GOSSIP

MORDECAI REFUSES TO KNEEL.

"Mordecai, you know as well as I do that Haman is simply hungry for power," Joseph insisted. "He'll be telling King Xerxes what to do before long."

Mordecai nodded his head. Unfortunately, what Joseph said was probably true. Mordecai had never understood why Xerxes preferred Haman over all the other royal officials. There was no denying that he had a strong influence on the king. Many people thought he even gave orders that the king did not know about.

Joseph continued talking. "I heard that the king has ordered all the royal officials to kneel and honor Haman when he passes by."

Mordecai stiffened up. "I will not do that. I will give the king the respect he deserves, but I cannot honor a man who hates my people."

"Then there's going to be trouble, Mordecai," Joseph warned. "It's common knowledge that Haman already has a grudge against you."

Mordecai kept his word. Day after day, he refused to kneel down or honor Haman. All the other officials obeyed the king's order that Haman be honored, and they watched Mordecai carefully to see if he would change his mind.

"Mordecai, you must kneel when Haman passes by," they said.

"I will not honor Haman," he answered.

"But it is the king's command," they countered. "When you do not honor Haman, you disobey the king."

When they questioned him, Mordecai would only repeat, "I will not honor Haman."

When word reached Haman that Mordecai would not kneel in his honor, he was enraged. "How dare he disobey the king's command!" Haman marched angrily through the halls of

"MORDECAI MUST BE PUNISHED."

the palace scheming to punish Mordecai for his actions. His assistant almost had to run to keep up with him.

"It would be simple enough to ask the king to have Mordecai hanged from the gallows," one of his assistants suggested. "It would be an example, in case there are others who decide they do not wish to honor you."

"Yes, yes, a very good idea," answered Haman. "But Mordecai is a Jew. If he can cause this sort of trouble, will there not be others who will do the same? Perhaps we can find a way to get rid of all the Jews."

"A brilliant idea, sir! The Jews could rise up and cause trouble for the king at any time. Mordecai may become their leader. It is best to be rid of them."

"I am sure I can get Xerxes to agree that the Jews are a threat and should be removed,"

Haman said confidently. "We must decide when and how. We shall cast the pur[1] and let the fates decide the date."

The date was set for eleven months away. "Good," said Haman with satisfaction. "That will give us plenty of time to persuade the king and make all the arrangements. We want to be sure we are thorough." They continued their discussions for several days until Haman had decided exactly what he would say to King Xerxes.

As soon as he had an opportunity, Haman spoke to Xerxes. "My good king," he said, "the king is a generous and powerful man. But we must be on the alert for threats to the king's power. There is a certain group of people scattered throughout the kingdom who may cause trouble. Their customs are different from ours,

---

[1]Pur is the Hebrew word for "lot."

CASTING THE PUR

and they do not obey the king's commands. I believe that it would be in the king's best interest to destroy these people so that the kingdom may remain strong."

Haman paused to judge the king's response.

"Continue," said the king.

"If it pleases the king," Haman said, "let a decree be issued to destroy them. I will put a great sum of money into the royal treasury for the men who carry out this command."

Xerxes lifted his hand and removed the signet ring from his finger and gave it to Haman. "Haman, you are my highest official. I know you are loyal, and I trust your judgment. You may write up this decree and seal it with my ring so that it becomes law. But keep the money and do with the people as you please."

Haman excitedly hurried back to his own rooms where his assistants were waiting for

PERSUADING THE KING

him. "That was even easier than I thought it would be," he said. He pulled out the royal signet ring and held it up for them to see. "We just got what we wanted, and it will not cost us anything. Now let's get organized!"

Immediately, Haman's assistants sent for the royal secretaries, and he began dictating the decree which would make it lawful for Persians to kill the Jews and steal their belongings. The secretaries worked day and night without relief. Haman was pressing to be sure the decree was drawn up before Xerxes could change his mind. He would often hold the royal ring in his hand and feel himself filled with the power it represented.

There were more than a hundred provinces in the kingdom and many different languages. Haman made sure that the governor of each province would receive the orders in the proper language. He called in translators to be sure that everything was exactly right. One day was chosen as the day when all the Jews could be killed. All the people of the kingdom were urged to be good citizens and obey the king's command. There was plenty of time for the decree to be delivered to the provinces and for the Persians to prepare to carry it out. Haman personally sealed each copy of the decree with the powerful royal ring of Xerxes, making it a law which could not be revoked.

Satisfied that all was in order, Haman called for the royal couriers. These young men would race to the far corners of the kingdom with copies of the new law. The proud official watched as his assistants handed out the copies and sent the couriers off on their journeys, urging them to go as quickly as possible.

Haman was already deciding how he would

DICTATING THE DEATH DECREE

DELIVERING THE DECREE

personally be sure that Mordecai was killed. Once again, he held up the royal ring and gloated as it sparkled in the light.

5

THE NEW LAW

The crowd gathering in the street grew larger and larger as more and more people stopped to watch the old man tearing his clothes and wailing loudly and bitterly.

"What's he doing?" someone asked.

"He's a Jew," someone else answered. "It's a funny custom they have, I suppose."

Laughter rippled through the crowd as

"HE'S A JEW!"

people joked about the strange man, who seemed unaware of the audience pressing in around him.

"I think it has something to do with the king's decree about the Jews," someone suggested. "I saw some other Jews behaving this way—but at least they stayed in their own homes instead of making a public spectacle in the middle of the street."

Joseph nudged his way through the crowd until he could see what was going on. He gasped when he realized who the man was. "Mordecai," he said aloud, without realizing it.

"Joseph, haven't you heard the king's command? How can you stay in the marketplace selling vegetables when Haman is plotting to destroy our people?" demanded Mordecai as he continued to rip his cloak and moan with grief.

Joseph reached out for Mordecai. "Please, my friend, why don't we find a place to sit down

"HAMAN IS PLOTTING TO DESTROY OUR PEOPLE."

and talk about this?" Joseph was whispering. He did not want to embarrass himself, but he could not abandon his old friend in the street.

Mordecai pushed Joseph off roughly. "Get away!" he shouted. "If you do not feel the horror of the crime which is being done to our people, then you are no friend of mine." Mordecai began to move up the street toward the city square in front of the king's gate. Some of the crowd lost interest and went on their way, but many people followed Mordecai, still amused by his odd behavior. Joseph moved along with the crowd, trying desperately to think of some way to make Mordecai stop before there was more trouble.

As they neared the palace, some of the guards and servants came out to watch. At last Joseph saw someone he recognized. "Please, hurry and tell the queen that her cousin is almost naked in

SACKCLOTH AND ASHES

the street," Joseph told the servant urgently. "Perhaps she can convince him to listen to reason."

When Esther heard the news, she acted quickly. She gathered some clothes together and gave them to a servant. "Hathach, take these clothes to Mordecai. Tell him I have sent them so that he will not disgrace himself." Anxiously, she watched from a window to see what was happening in the street below. Mordecai was continuing to tear his clothes to shreds and cry out loudly with every rip as if he were in pain.

"I have no need to cover myself," shouted Mordecai when the clothes were given to him. "Tell Esther that she should join my mourning, rather than trying to make me stop."

Hathach the servant obediently reported Mordecai's words to the queen, who leaned further out the window to watch her cousin while trying to decide what to do.

"Hathach," she said, "please find out exactly what my cousin is mourning and why he is behaving this way. Ask him what he wants from me."

This time Hathach was gone a long time. Esther could see Mordecai gesturing and waving around a piece of parchment. Even the full beard covering his features did not hide the redness of anger in Mordecai's face. *If only I could speak to him personally,* Esther thought. Perhaps then she could understand his distress. Had something tragic happened in their street? Had something gone wrong with his work? But Mordecai would not be allowed any nearer to the palace while he insisted on wearing sackcloth and wailing loudly. Esther would have to depend on Hathach to carry accurate messages back and forth until the problem could be sorted out. What did that scrap of parchment mean? From what Esther

HOLDING UP THE PARCHMENT

could see, Mordecai's anger seemed to focus on what was written there.

At last Hathach returned.

"What is it, Hathach? What is my cousin so upset about?"

"It is the king's new law, my queen," the servant said humbly.

"What law? The king makes laws every day. What is special about this one?"

"Your cousin says that Haman has organized a plan to destroy the Jewish people, and the king has given his consent."

"Destroy the Jewish people?" Esther echoed in disbelief. "Why would my husband make such an order? The Jews have not been troublesome to his kingdom."

"I cannot say, my queen. But the decree has been sealed with the royal ring and sent out to all the provinces. Mordecai has a copy. I saw it myself. On a certain day, it will be lawful for Persians to kill the Jews and plunder their goods."

Now Esther fully understood Mordecai's distress. Four years had passed since she had been made queen, and still Xerxes did not know that she was Jewish. If he had known, would it have influenced his decision? Surely she would be safe within the palace—but what about Mordecai? She knew Haman hated her cousin. Mordecai's life was certainly in danger.

"I have none of the king's power, Hathach," Esther said. "What does my cousin think I can do?"

"He begs you to go to the king and beg for mercy for the Jewish people."

"But if the decree has been sealed with the royal ring, then it has already been made into law. I cannot change that!"

Hathach was silent, knowing that his role

HATHACH TELLS QUEEN ESTHER THE NEWS.

was merely that of a servant and a messenger, not an advisor to the queen. Esther wished he would speak, but he did not. She grieved for what would happen to Mordecai and the rest of her people. But what could she possibly do? She had no authority to reverse his decree, and she felt she would have very little influence on his decision.

"This is what I want you to tell my cousin," Esther said at last. "Remind him that all the king's officials and the people of the royal provinces know that for any man or woman who approaches the king in the inner court without being summoned, the king has but one law: That person will be put to death. The only exception to this is for the king to extend the gold scepter and spare the person's life. But it has been more than thirty days since the king has called for me. If I go to him without being summoned, the law will apply to me also."

SORTING OUT HER THOUGHTS

Esther was frightened and desperate. Perhaps Mordecai was right; perhaps she was the only hope the Jews had. But what good could she do if she were put to death?

"There must be another way! Tell Mordecai that I cannot go to the king!"

6

ESTHER'S DECISION

Mordecai looked up and saw the slight figure of Esther peering out the window. There was no question that she had grown into a lovely woman, as he had always known she would. For years, he had been sad because of their separation and because Esther could not enjoy a normal life among her people. Xerxes could have had any Persian woman he wanted. Mordecai had never

LOOKING TO ESTHER FOR HELP

understood why Jewish girls had been rounded up during the search for a new queen. But now—perhaps this was exactly the reason Esther had been chosen as queen. Perhaps God Himself had done the choosing, and not merely Xerxes.

Even though she was the queen and lived inside the palace, Esther did not always know very much about the king's business, especially where Haman was involved. So it was quite possible that she truly did not know about the new law and the reason why Mordecai was wailing in the street. When she found out what was written on the parchment he held tightly in his hand, she would be as angry as he was. He was sure of that. Although she had not lived among the Jews for nearly eight years now, Mordecai simply could not believe that Esther would turn her back on them. Surely once she understood the seriousness of the circumstances, she would do everything in

MORDECAI AWAITING ESTHER'S DECISION

her power to save her own people.

When Hathach returned with Esther's message saying that she could not go to the king, Mordecai listened carefully and then raised his eyes toward Esther's window in disbelief and disappointment. For a moment he was overcome with helplessness and personal sorrow. Esther had allowed her own fear to rob her of the courage she needed to rise to this challenge. But Mordecai would not give up.

"I have one more message for the queen, Hathach. Listen carefully, and give her this message exactly: Do not think that because you are in the king's house you alone of all the Jews will escape. For if you remain silent at this time, relief and deliverance for the Jews will arise from another place, but you and your father's family will perish. And who knows but that you have come to your royal position for such a time as this?"

SENDING A WARNING TO ESTHER

"What does he mean, Hathach?" Esther demanded when she received Mordecai's message.

"It is not for me to say, my queen. I have given you the message exactly as it was given to me. I can do no more."

"Of course not. Please wait outside my door. I will call you when I have prepared an answer for my cousin."

Esther was left alone in her room. She looked around at the luxury which surrounded her: more clothes than she would ever wear, the most epensive perfumes, cosmetic creams to keep her youthful and lovely, a choice of couches for lounging or eating when trays of gourmet foods were carried in to her by one of the many servants who waited on her every moment of the day. Full drapes with delicately twisted gold braid adorned her windows. She slept on a bed filled with the softest feathers and covered with the finest fabrics in the kingdom. If she wanted something, she simply rang a bell and a servant appeared to satisfy her wish. She was respected and honored as the queen by everyone in the palace.

Yet Mordecai's message implied that even she would not be safe inside the palace. He was right, of course. Although the king himself did not know she was Jewish, many other people did. She could not be certain she would survive the day that the decree was carried out.

It struck her that she had nothing to lose by approaching the king. He might order her death, but she would surely lose her life in a few months anyway. And if he extended the gold scepter to her, she might be able to find a way to help her people. Perhaps now was the time to tell Xerxes that she was among the people he had ordered killed. She had nothing to lose and everything to gain—for herself and her people.

ALONE IN LUXURY

PRAYING

She spun around and raced to her door, calling, "Hathach! Hathach!"

"Tell Mordecai this," she said triumphantly. "Go, gather together all the Jews who are in Susa and fast for me. Do not eat or drink for three days, night or day. I and my maids will fast as you do. When this is done, I will go to the king, even though it is against the law. And if I perish, I perish."

Esther ran back to the window and watched as her message was delivered. A smile began to cross Mordecai's face, and then it broke into a full grin. He looked up at her with pride and gratitude beaming from his features. Then she knew she had made the right choice.

Just as she instructed, for three days and three nights, Esther and her maids and all the Jewish people in the city of Susa had nothing to eat or drink. They prayed constantly for Esther

"TELL MORDECAI THAT I WILL GO TO THE KING."

and the challenge she was about to face. Everyone understood how important it was to all of them for the queen to succeed.

Esther had many moments of doubt and fear. More than once she was tempted to send a message to Mordecai saying that she could not carry out her promise. When she slept, she dreamed of the moment when she would approach the king. Sometimes in her dream he would hold out the gold scepter in approval; other times he did not, and she would wake up screaming with terror. During the day, Esther sat in her high window looking out into the streets. She did not know many people in the city any more, but she knew that many of them were Jews whose lives were in danger. She prayed harder and more intensely for courage and strength.

On the third morning, Esther dressed carefully. She had made thorough preparations for

DREAMS AND NIGHTMARES

this day. The time had come when she was thankful for her exquisite beauty. Perhaps it would be her loveliness that would make the king extend his scepter and welcome her into his presence when he had not called for her. She put on her finest royal robes and used the perfume that she knew Xerxes liked. Trembling with every step she took, she walked through the palace and stood in the inner court, where King Xerxes was sitting on his throne. It was dangerous enough to be there at all; she could not risk speaking. She would have to wait until he looked up and saw her standing there, and hope that he would be pleased with what he saw.

Esther tried to smile and look relaxed, but her eyes were drawn to the gold scepter at the king's side. She was startled when Xerxes looked up and spoke.

PREPARING TO SEE THE KING

"Queen Esther! I do not remember that I called for you."

Esther was still watching the gold scepter. It did not move.

7

A Special Banquet

Esther held her breath for what seemed like
hours, waiting to see if Xerxes would lift his
scepter and point it toward her.

At last his hand moved toward his side, and
she saw the glint of gold as the scepter was
raised. To her relief, the expression on his face
was soft and gentle.

"What is it, Queen Esther?" he asked. "What

"WHAT IS IT, QUEEN ESTHER?"

is your request? I will give you up to half my kingdom."

Xerxes had said those words to Esther many times in the four years they had been married. Never had she asked anything of him, and certainly not half his kingdom! In the three days she had spent fasting and praying, she had pictured this moment in her mind often. What would she say to the king? Was this the right moment to reveal her Jewish background? Should she fall on her face and beg for mercy? She had planned what she would say, but all of a sudden she wanted to turn around and run from the room.

Esther swallowed once and tried to speak. Her voice hardly sounded like it was hers, but the words she heard were the ones she had rehearsed. "If it pleases the king," she said, "let the king, together with Haman, come today to a banquet I have prepared for him."

SPEAKING WITH THE KING

The king smiled widely. "A banquet with my lovely queen—what a wonderful idea. I have been so busy with the affairs of the kingdom that I have not seen my wife for weeks." Xerxes turned to the servant standing near him. "Bring Haman at once, so that we may do what Queen Esther asks."

The king stood up and offered his arm to Esther. She smiled and laid her hand on his arm, and they left the room together.

When they entered the banquet hall, the queen once again held her breath while she awaited the king's reaction. She had planned an elaborate banquet with fine meats, fresh breads, juicy fruits, and crisp vegetables. Everything was laid out attractively on a long table covered with a sparkling white linen tablecloth. There was much more food than three people could possibly eat in one day. The colors and textures of the foods

THE BANQUET HALL

"YOU HAVE DONE WELL."

blended together perfectly, like an artist's painting, and the fragrances rising from the steaming dishes were irresistible. Three low couches covered with silk in regal colors were grouped in front of the table for Xerxes, Esther, and Haman to lounge on while they enjoyed the feast. A dozen servants stood ready to serve them with gold plates and wine goblets.

"You have done well, Queen Esther," said Xerxes. "I will be pleased to sit at your banquet."

Esther smiled in relief and began to relax. By the time Haman entered the room, she felt confident that her plan might indeed work. She would please the king in every way possible, even including Haman in the festivities, and then she would make her request on behalf of her people.

The three of them feasted for nearly three hours. Servants brought to them a steady stream of fresh plates heaped with a wide variety of

HAMAN GAZING AT ESTHER ODDLY

food and poured wine freely from the many jugs Esther had arranged for. Xerxes and Haman talked at length about business matters, while Esther smiled and made sure that the king continued to be pleased. She was alert for any mention of Haman's cruel plan against the Jews, but it was not discussed. Often she felt Haman looking at her in an odd way. She met his gaze with ease and confidence, but she could not help wondering what he was thinking about. Was he planning how he would kill her along with Mordecai? Was he suspicious about why she had invited him to this special banquet?

At last Xerxes turned his attention to Esther. He reached for her slender hand and pulled her to his side.

"Now what is it you really want, Esther?" he asked. "Surely you did not risk coming into the inner court without being called simply to invite me to a banquet. Whatever you want, I will give it to you, up to half of my kingdom."

The moment had come for Esther to decide what to say. Haman was looking at her. Clearly, he was also very curious about what Esther's words might be. In a fleeting moment, Esther had to judge the king's state of mind and answer his question.

"My petition and request is this," she said. "If the king regards me with favor and it pleases the king to grant my petition and fulfill my request, let the king and Haman come tomorrow to the banquet I will prepare for them. Then I will answer the king's question."

"Very well," said Xerxes. "You make me very curious, Queen Esther. This has been a wonderful banquet today, and I will look forward to another exquisite feast tomorrow."

Haman bowed his head to Esther. "I am

flattered that the queen would invite me to a banquet such as this. I will be honored to be the queen's guest once again tomorrow."

The two men left the banquet hall. Esther let out a sigh and collapsed back onto her couch. Although the room was very warm, she was trembling. What would happen if the king changed his mind and did not come to her banquet tomorrow? Had she missed her chance to speak to him about what was really on her mind? Had she made the wrong choice when she decided to wait another day?

Esther refused to let her fear overcome her. She had promised Mordecai she would speak to the king on behalf of her people. As frightened as she was, she knew that she was the one person in the kingdom who was in a position to help the Jews.

Abruptly, she stood up and called the servants

PART ONE OF HER PLAN WAS COMPLETE.

in the room to her. "We will make another banquet for the king tomorrow," she said. "It will be even more beautiful than today, with more of the king's favorite foods. I will select the food myself. We will have the royal musicians come in and play music that pleases the king. If the king wishes to dance, we will dance."

The rest of the day was spent planning for the second banquet. At last, weary from a busy day, Esther returned to her own room. Out of habit, she moved to the window and looked out. She had not seen Mordecai during the three days of fasting and praying, and she did not really expect to see him now. Nevertheless, she longed to sit with him as she had when she was a little girl and feel the comfort that would come from his presence.

The streets were quiet at the end of the day. Esther thought of her own little street in the

REFLECTING ON HER LIFE

Jewish corner of the city and wished that she could once again move freely from house to house with Rebekah and her other friends. But those days were gone. And after all these years of life in the palace, Esther was beginning to understand that there was a reason why she had been taken from the marketplace that morning eight years earlier.

8

THE GALLOWS

Haman left the palace whistling that day. What a feast! And what an honor to have been invited to dine alone with the royal couple. If the queen herself showed him such respect, he surely deserved the honor of the other royal officials kneeling down when he passed by. When he walked through the gate, Haman nodded at the officers who had replaced Bigthana and Teresh.

MORDECAI WOULD NOT BOW.

Nearby was Mordecai, just finishing his work for the day. Haman paused slightly to give Mordecai an opportunity to honor him.

Mordecai lifted his eyes briefly, then went about his business without acknowledging Haman's presence. Immediately, Haman's good mood disappeared, and he was filled with rage. No matter what other honors he received, he was overcome with anger whenever he thought of Mordecai and how this one man refused to bow to him. Haman held his tongue, however. The king's decree had been sent to all the provinces, and Haman would have his revenge in only a few months.

Haman strolled the streets to his spacious and luxurious home in a wealthy part of Susa. He was greeted by his wife, Zeresh, and several friends who were visiting.

"Our meal will be ready in a few minutes,

Haman," Zeresh said. "I have instructed the servants to prepare your favorite foods tonight."

"My dear wife, I am afraid that I have no appetite," Haman answered.

"But why not?"

Haman lifted his head proudly. "I have been to a banquet hosted by the queen."

Zeresh shrugged her shoulders. "You have been to many royal banquets."

"That's right," said one of Haman's friends. "You are always boasting to us about the exotic foods you eat at the palace."

Haman smiled. "This one was different. This was a very private meal. The king and I were the only guests invited by the queen."

Haman looked around and saw that his wife and guests were impressed.

"My career has been successful beyond any dreams I ever had," Haman bragged. "In only a

BOASTING TO HIS WIFE AND FRIENDS

few short years, the king has promoted me above all the other royal officials and entrusted me with important responsibilities. He discusses things with me that he talks about to no one else. It is almost as if we are ruling the kingdom together."

"You have worked very hard, my husband," Zeresh said. "You have deserved every honor you have received."

"The king has even entrusted me with his signet ring. I have the authority to declare laws in his name."

"Haman, I have known you for many years," said his friend. "You have always been very fair. The king is wise to trust you. It was only fitting that he should command the other officials to pay honor to you."

The smile was wiped from Haman's face and replaced by a scowl.

"I would be a happy man if it were not for

that Jew, Mordecai," he said. "The king has honored me; the queen has invited me to another banquet tomorrow. Yet I am not satisfied because when I walk past Mordecai, he refuses to acknowledge my position. I cannot stand to see him at the king's gate acting as if he were more important than I am."

"Then why don't you do something about it?" Zeresh said.

"Yes," said their friend. "You just said you have the authority of the king's ring. Why not go to the king tomorrow morning and ask that Mordecai be hanged? Then you can enjoy your banquet with the queen without thinking about that man ever again."

Haman was nodding. Perhaps this was a good idea. He would not have to wait until the day his new law would be carried out. Mordecai was openly disobeying the king's command to

"MORDECAI REFUSES TO ACKNOWLEDGE MY POSITION."

honor Haman. This was already against the law, so why not have him hanged now?

"You can have the gallows built tonight," his wife suggested. "Make it very high—seventy-five feet—so that everyone can see what happens to a man who does not honor my worthy husband."

Haman's face showed his pleasure once again. "You are true friends and a dear wife. I will do as you have suggested. Please, go in and dine on the meal my wife has prepared. I will take care of the details of the gallows and join you later."

"HAVE THE GALLOWS BUILT TONIGHT!"

9

XERXES HONORS MORDECAI

Xerxes could not sleep. He punched at his pillows, threw the covers off, pulled them back on again, turned over to his back, laid on one side, then the other—nothing worked. He simply could not sleep that night. Perhaps it was too much rich food from Esther's banquet keeping him awake. Whatever the reason for his sleeplessness, it was very late when he grew frustrated and

THE KING COULD NOT SLEEP.

READING THE OFFICIAL RECORDS

rang the bell for his personal attendant to come.

The servant entered with a lamp in his hand. "What is the king's wish?"

"I cannot sleep. Go find the official records of my reign and read to me."

The attendant read for hours and hours. Although he was having difficulty staying awake himself, the king showed no signs of going to sleep, so the reading continued. They came to the portion of the official record which retold the story of how Mordecai had exposed Bigthana and Teresh, the guards who had plotted to kill the king.

The king was sitting upright, wide awake. He had completely forgotten this incident until now. As the attendant began to read about another subject, King Xerxes interrupted.

"What honor and recognition has Mordecai received for this?" he asked.

The servant looked again at the writing in front of him, searching for an answer to the king's question. "Nothing has been done for him."

Xerxes got out of bed and glanced toward the window, where daylight was peeking in. "Who is in the court this morning?"

The attendant hurriedly asked another servant. "I am told that Haman has just arrived, my king," he said. "He was hoping to have a word with you this morning."

"Bring him in," Xerxes ordered.

Haman entered very quickly, pleased that the king had agreed to see him so early in the morning and in his private chambers.

"Haman," Xerxes said, "what should be done for the man the king delights to honor?"

Of course, he means me, Haman thought to himself. *I will wait to speak to him about Mordecai another day.* He thought carefully before

HAMAN BEFORE THE KING

he spoke. Perhaps if he asked for something other than wealth, the king would be flattered. Aloud, Haman said, "For the man the king delights to honor, have them bring a royal robe the king has worn and a horse the king has ridden, one with a royal crest placed on its head. Then let the robe and horse be entrusted to one of the king's most noble princes. Let them robe the man the king delights to honor and lead him on the horse through the city streets, proclaiming before him, 'This is what is done for the man the king delights to honor.'"

Haman was already picturing himself astride a royal horse, wearing a robe which the king himself had worn. For a moment, he was able to forget about Mordecai and enjoy the honor the king intended to give him.

"Go at once," the king commanded Haman. "Get the robe and the horse and do just as you

DESCRIBING A ROYAL REWARD

have suggested. Do this for Mordecai the Jew, who sits at the king's gate. Be sure not to neglect anything you have recommended. It is a perfect plan."

Haman hardly knew what to say. "Yes, my king." The thought of having to honor Mordecai made him feel sick. He wondered what he had done to displease the king that would make him deserve this humiliation.

Xerxes sighed contentedly. "I have been up all night, Haman, but I believe I can sleep now. Don't forget about Queen Esther's banquet. I will see you there."

Haman had been dismissed. But there were witnesses to what the king had commanded. Haman had no choice but to carry out the plan he had described when he thought he was the one to be honored.

Angrily, Haman went to the king's dressing

"BRING THE ROYAL REWARD TO MORDECAI."

HAMAN GRUDGINGLY HONORS MORDECAI.

room and selected a royal robe, one which he had seen the king wearing only a few days ago. He carried this with him to the royal stables and chose a horse which the king had ridden only once. The crest which indicated that this was the king's horse was placed on the animal's head, and Haman led the way to where he knew he would find Mordecai.

Mordecai looked up from his work. "Haman, even with a horse and a royal crest, you are not worthy of my honor."

A crowd had gathered at the unusual sight of Haman standing before Mordecai with one of the king's horses. Haman heard some snickering from deep within the crowd but forced himself not to turn around and look.

"The horse is for you, Mordecai, along with this royal robe sent from King Xerxes for you to wear."

"Is this some kind of joke, Haman?" Mordecai demanded. "Why would the king send a horse and a robe for me to wear? I have never even spoken to him."

"Apparently he believes you saved his life." Haman had to force out every word.

"So I did," said Mordecai with conviction.

"The king wishes to honor you for that deed." Haman held open the robe for Mordecai.

Mordecai was still not sure what to believe. After a brief hesitation, he stepped forward and allowed Haman to wrap the robe around him and help him mount the horse. To Mordecai's surprise, Haman himself took the reins of the horse and led him through the streets. On every block, he cried out, "This is what is done for the man the king delights to honor."

A crowd gathered on nearly every corner. Haman and Mordecai were both well-known

COVERED IN SHAME

men, and their hatred for each other had been obvious for a long time. Cheers and boos were heard in response to the sight of the king's highest official leading the horse of a Jew.

At last, completely humiliated, Haman returned Mordecai to his place outside the palace. Haman himself ran home as quickly as he could.

"What is it, Haman?" asked Zeresh, alarmed that her husband should come home in the middle of the day. "You look terrible! What happened to you?"

"Haman, my friend," said his guest, "you are covered with dust and sweat. What in the world have you been doing?"

Haman covered his face in shame and grief. He did not answer their questions for a long time. But he knew that word would reach them soon enough, so he began to tell them what had happened that morning.

"I went to the palace early to see the king, as you suggested," he said. "I was delighted when he called me into his private chambers. But before I could ask his permission to hang Mordecai, the king was asking me what should be done to a man the king wished to honor."

Haman stopped and shook his head sadly. "I have been such a fool. I thought he meant me! I thought he wanted to give me further honor, so I suggested a royal robe and a royal horse. Then I found out he meant Mordecai! I went to see the king this morning because I want to hang Mordecai for not honoring me. Instead, the king ordered me to honor Mordecai by walking through the streets while Mordecai rode a royal horse. The whole city has seen me. I am ruined!"

The once proud Haman collapsed on a couch and covered his face with his hands. "How can

"YOU HAVE BEEN HUMILIATED."

I possibly go back and face the king now? I will not be able to walk through the streets without people sneering at me."

Sadly, Zeresh agreed. "You have been publicly humiliated by a Jew. If only you had spoken to the king sooner about Mordecai—this would never have happened."

Haman, Zeresh, and their guest sat together in silence, sharing the grief of the official's shame. After a long time, they were interrupted by the soft knock of a servant.

"Yes?" said Zeresh.

"The king's servant has arrived to remind Haman of the queen's banquet."

Haman once again hid his face in his hands.

10

THE PLOT REVEALED

Esther was ready for Haman and Xerxes to enter the banquet hall. She had slept very little the night before. Instead, she had spent the hours praying and begging God for courage and mercy. Still nervous about what she faced, she felt braver than she had since she first committed herself to this plan.

She moved through the hall inspecting the

LAST-MINUTE INSPECTION

A BANQUET FIT FOR A KING

preparations and was very satisfied. The gold plates and goblets sparkled in the bright light coming in through the windows. Fresh flowers from the palace gardens adorned the tables. The food had been prepared perfectly. She had made sure that everything the king liked best was on the menu and prepared personally by the chief palace cook. Skilled musicians stood by with trumpets and lyres to fill the hall with the king's favorite music. The couches were lined with soft pillows for the king's comfort, and the servants were ready to do whatever the queen directed.

When Haman arrived, Esther thought that he looked very tired. She had not heard about the embarrassment he had suffered that morning, but she sensed that something was wrong with him. He seemed even more eager than usual to please King Xerxes, but Esther did not believe that his smile was sincere. Yesterday he had been

ENJOYING THE MEAL

lighthearted and proud. Today he acted very nervous and discouraged.

The meal went very well. To Esther's relief, the king seemed pleased with everything she had selected and ate heartily. Xerxes and Haman joked and laughed together, and the king often smiled at his wife as they spent the entire afternoon eating. Esther was nervous, but she felt encouraged that the feast was going so well. *Haman is acting a bit odd*, she thought, but she could not be distracted by worrying about the king's high official. There was a purpose for this banquet, and she must remember it at every moment.

At the end of the meal, when none of them could eat anything more, the king signaled for more wine and settled back comfortably on his couch.

"And now, my queen," Xerxes said, "you

must tell me about your request. You may have anything you wish, up to half of my kingdom."

Esther knew the moment had come; she could delay no further. Everything had gone according to plan up to this point, and she prayed quickly and silently that what she was about to say would be well received by the king.

"If I have found favor with you, O King, and if it pleases Your Majesty, grant me my life—this is my petition. And spare my people—this is my request." Esther kept her eyes fixed on Xerxes as she spoke, resisting the temptation to look at Haman for his reaction. "For I and my people have been sold for destruction and slaughter and annihilation. If we had merely been sold as male and female slaves, I would have kept quiet, because that would not justify disturbing the king."

Xerxes sat up straight on the edge of his couch. "What are you talking about, Queen

ESTHER TELLS THE KING HER REQUEST.

Esther? What do you mean, you have been sold for destruction and slaughter?"

"I am Jewish, O King."

The king continued to look puzzled.

"A law has been issued with the king's signet ring to destroy my people."

"Who has done this?" Xerxes demanded. "Where is the man who has dared to do such a thing?"

Esther now turned her head toward Haman. She struggled to keep her voice from breaking. "Our enemy is this man, Haman."

"The Jews, Haman?" Xerxes shouted. "You want to destroy the Jews? You told me there were people who would be a threat to my power. The Jews are no such threat!"

Haman was visibly frightened. He, too, was sitting on the edge of his couch. He stuttered as he began to speak. "I. . .I. . .I was only

"OUR ENEMY IS HAMAN."

"YOU WANT TO DESTROY THE JEWS?"

trying to do what is best for the kingdom, Your Majesty."

"You tricked me! You used my signet ring for your own purposes, and now this horrible idea has been made into law."

Esther had never seen the king so angry. His eyes bulged, and his face was flaming red. His loud shouting echoed throughout the banquet hall, and the sound magnified his rage. The servants, who had been quietly clearing the table, now stood still as they watched the king. Xerxes stomped over to the table and set his wine goblet down very hard. Then he turned on his heel and left the hall through the door that led to the palace gardens, his royal robes flapping briskly behind him.

For a very long moment, Esther and Haman stared at each other while a dozen servants looked on. No one in the room moved.

PLEADING FOR HIS LIFE

Encouraged by the king's anger, Esther now felt she had the upper hand. She straightened her shoulders and spoke confidently. "I believe our banquet has come to an end, Haman. You may leave. I am sure the king will call for you when he is ready to see you."

Haman lurched toward Esther. "Queen Esther, this has all been a misunderstanding," he said. "Please allow me to explain. . . ."

Esther put up her hand to stop Haman. "You will come no closer to the queen."

"I am begging for my life, my queen. You alone can spare me." Haman was very desperate and looked as if he might even cry. "I plead for your royal mercy, Queen Esther. Spare my life."

Esther looked at Haman without sympathy. "I know that you hate my cousin, Haman. In fact, you hate all my people, even me. How is it that you, who have no mercy in you, should dare to plead with the queen for mercy for your own life?"

Although she was very tense about this encounter with Haman, Esther had remained on the couch, trying to appear in control. Haman once again moved toward her—and this time he lost his balance and toppled on top of the queen.

"Get off!" she screamed. "How dare you!" Then she heard an angry shout.

"Haman!" King Xerxes had entered the banquet hall once again, just as Haman fell on top of Esther. He rushed across the empty room and roughly grabbed Haman by the hair and pulled him off Esther. He turned the official around and roared directly into his face. "Will you even stoop so low as to attack the queen? You are a greater fool than I, Haman. Get out of my sight!"

"GET OUT OF MY SIGHT!"

King Xerxes pushed Haman into the waiting arms of soldiers who had followed the king in and now had their swords drawn, standing ready for the king's command. It was obvious to all that Haman was doomed to die.

The king's personal attendant, who had served Xerxes for many years, stepped forward to speak to the king. "Your Majesty, if it please the king, Haman has this very morning built a high gallows at his own home. He was intending to hang Mordecai the Jew."

"Hang him on it," Xerxes thundered.

11

A New Decree

"I did it, Cousin! I did it!" Esther rushed excitedly into Mordecai's arms as if she were a little girl. "Haman will cause us no more trouble. Now that the king knows you are my cousin, you will be welcome in the palace whenever we want to see each other."

Mordecai laughed at Esther's excitement. "I am very proud of my beautiful cousin! I was

"I DID IT, COUSIN!"

confident at every moment that you would do the right thing."

They sat together in the palace gardens, one of Esther's favorite places. Mordecai had never been permitted to come to this part of the palace before, but he could see now why Esther loved to sit in the garden. It was truly lovely and very restful. He hoped that they would have many more visits in this pleasant setting.

Esther laid her head on Mordecai's shoulder. "I am so glad that ordeal is over," she said. "I'm not sure I could have held on much longer. Just being in the same room with Haman made me so nervous!"

"My dear cousin, you did a wonderful job," Mordecai said proudly. "Without your courage, our people would be without hope. But the ordeal is not over. It has only begun."

Abruptly, Esther sat up and looked Mordecai

in the eye. "What do you mean, Cousin?"

Mordecai spoke calmly and quietly. "Esther, you have grown up under Persian rule. I am sure you know the nature of Persian law."

For a moment, Esther did not speak. Then she put into words what her cousin had reminded her of. "Once a decree has been made into law, it cannot be reversed."

"That is correct," Mordecai said sadly. "Haman may be gone, but his plan remains law. Our people still face the day of execution."

"But I spoke to the king—" Esther protested.

Mordecai interrupted her. "Even the king cannot reverse a law."

"Then what more can we do?" Esther asked desperately. "We are no better off than before."

"You must speak to the king again, Esther."

"For what purpose, Cousin?"

"The king cannot change the law, but he

"THE KING CANNOT REVERSE A LAW."

"YOU MUST SPEAK TO THE KING AGAIN."

can make a new decree which would allow us to defend ourselves."

Esther shook her head sadly. "There will still be a great deal of Jewish bloodshed."

Mordecai nodded. "Perhaps. Or it might be that the knowledge that we are prepared to defend ourselves will discourage our attackers from doing as Haman wished."

"You are very wise, Cousin. Why my husband chose to promote Haman and not you is something I do not understand."

Mordecai smiled. "And you are very sweet. But we must find a way to speak to the king. Do you think he will call for you soon?"

"I never know. After what happened with Haman, perhaps he will want to see me again very soon."

"My queen," said the voice of a servant behind them.

Esther turned her head. "Yes?"

"The king wishes to see you in the inner court. He asks that your cousin come with you."

Esther and Mordecai looked at each other and grinned.

"This is your opportunity," Mordecai urged. "It would not be proper for me to speak to the king on this subject, but perhaps he would listen to his queen."

In the throne room, Xerxes greeted Esther and Mordecai warmly. "Do not be alarmed. I wish to welcome you and honor you for your deeds."

Mordecai bowed deeply before the king. "I am most honored to be in your presence. Allow me to express my gratitude for the royal robe and the royal horse presented to me earlier today."

"What a wonderful and terrible day we have all had," the king said. "In the morning, Mordecai was honored because he saved my

A WARM WELCOME

life. In the afternoon, Haman, my most trusted official, was hanged because he wished to destroy your people." The king turned to Esther. "I believe it would be proper for you to have Haman's property, Queen Esther. This represents a great deal of money. I am sure you will find a wise use for it."

"Thank you, Your Majesty. If it pleases the king, I wish for my cousin to be given charge over the money. He is wiser than I could ever hope to be."

"Very well. I will make the arrangements." Now Xerxes turned to Mordecai. "I have something else for you, Mordecai, something of far greater significance than a horse or a robe."

King Xerxes held up his signet ring and motioned for Mordecai to step forward to receive it. "I have trusted the wrong man for many years. From now on, I will trust the right man.

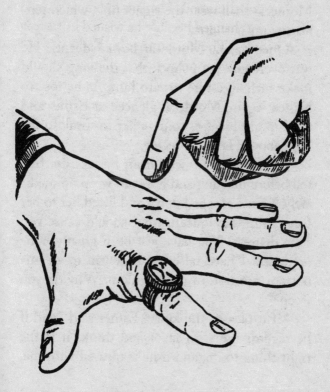

THE SIGNET RING

Mordecai shall wear the signet ring, which represents my authority."

Once again, Mordecai bowed deeply. He was overcome with shock that the king should make such a gesture toward him. As he rose to his feet again, Mordecai glanced at Esther and tried to use his eyes to urge her to speak to the king about Haman's decree.

Esther took her cue from her cousin. She fell before the king and began to weep. Immediately, Xerxes stooped down and lifted her to her feet again. "My queen, what should cause you such distress? You have just been greatly honored, and I have raised your cousin to an important position in my kingdom. Why do you weep?"

"If it pleases the king," Esther said, "and if he regards me with favor and thinks it is the right thing to do, and if he is pleased with me,

PLEADING WITH XERXES

let an order be written to overturn the law which Haman sent to all the provinces for the destruction of the Jews. For how can I bear to see such disaster fall on my people? How can I bear to see the destruction of my family?"

"I have already given this much thought, Queen Esther," the king assured her. "No document written in the king's name and sealed with his ring can be reversed. But we can write a new document." He turned to Mordecai. "I will leave it to your judgment to determine what this new document must say in order to protect your people. You may use the royal secretaries to write it and the couriers to carry it to the far corners of my kingdom. Use the signet ring I have given you, and this document shall also become law."

The royal secretaries were called immediately, and Mordecai set them to work very quickly. He had already planned what the document must

WRITING A NEW LAW

SEALING THE DECREE

say. The Jews in every city of the kingdom would have the right to band together and defend themselves against their enemies on the day which Haman had chosen to attack the Jews. They could form their own armies to protect their families and property from any armies which might attack them. Esther was right; there would be bloodshed, but at least the Jews would have the right to defend themselves.

Mordecai's new law was sent to every province in the kingdom. As the couriers left on their journeys, Mordecai looked on with deep satisfaction. His own rise in power was meaningless to him. The royal robes and the crown which the king had placed on his head were not important. His satisfaction came from knowing that Esther would be safe and that instead of wailing and grieving, there would be joy and gladness among the Jews throughout the kingdom.

12

God's Plan

"What are you working on, Cousin?" Esther walked happily into the room in the palace where her cousin now spent his days working for the king. She opened the drapes on the window to let in some fresh air. "Why do you always forget to open the windows when you come into this room?" she chided. "It is so much more pleasant when you let in some light and air."

LETTING IN LIGHT

Mordecai shrugged his shoulders. "I suppose I'm too busy. There is always so much work to do. I just never think about it." He put down his quill and rubbed his eyes with the heels of his hands. He had stayed at his writing table very late last night and had returned very early in the morning.

Eighteen months had passed since the final encounter with Haman. Even the awful day of destruction was behind them now. The Jews had organized and prepared well; they had been the victors in the skirmishes and battles occurring throughout the kingdom. Many more Persians were killed than Jews. Mordecai and Esther had been protected within the walls of the palace and guarded closely against any possible attack.

Xerxes had been very pleased with everything Mordecai had done for him during the

THE JEWS WERE VICTORIOUS IN BATTLE.

FAMILY AGAIN!

months since Haman's plot had been over-
thrown. Esther's humble cousin was rapidly taking on more authority and responsibility in the
kingdom.

Esther walked over to the table where her
cousin was bent over a parchment, once again
intent on his writing. Although he was concen-
trating, she did not hesitate to interrupt. She
knew he was always glad to see her, no matter
how busy he was.

"I'm so glad we can be together in the palace
now, Cousin. I know we can never get back the
eight years we were apart, but it is wonderful to
be able to see you every day."

Mordecai smiled in agreement. "It is because
of you that we are together now—because you
were willing to face an enormous challenge."

"I would never have done it if the challenge
had not come from you, Cousin. I knew that if

you thought I should do it, then it was the right thing."

"God was gracious to our people. He heard our prayers and answered our cries. We were honored to be His instruments."

Esther nodded. Her cousin expressed exactly what she felt. After a moment she repeated the question she had asked when she entered the room. "What are you working on?" She leaned over his shoulder to look at the parchment.

"I am very relieved to have Haman's wicked plan completely behind us," Mordecai answered. "But one thing still bothers me. If we try to forget the terrible part of those days, we will also forget the wonderful part. I do not want our people to forget the ordeal that we faced. We were victorious on the day of destruction planned by Haman, and we rejoice in God's deliverance." He gestured toward the words he

"GOD WAS GRACIOUS TO OUR PEOPLE."

had written. "I want all Jews throughout the kingdom to teach their children this story, so I am writing it down before I become too old to remember everything that happened. We must always remember the day that our sorrow was turned into joy, and the time that our mourning was changed into celebration.

Esther gently stroked her cousin's head. "Do you mean a feast, Cousin? Shall we have a feast to remember this deliverance, just as we celebrate the deliverance of the Passover when our people left Egypt?"

Mordecai was pleased with Esther's response. "That's exactly what I mean," he said enthusiastically. "I want us to have a holiday every year, two days of feasting and giving presents of food to one another and gifts to the poor. Every year on the anniversary of the day that Haman chose by casting lots, we will

"LET US HAVE A FEAST TO CELEBRATE DELIVERANCE."

remember that our lives do not belong to those who use the pur to make decisions. We are still God's people."

He paused and turned around in his chair. His face was bright with conviction.

"Esther, for many years, we did not understand why you had been taken from us, or why you had been chosen as queen," Mordecai continued. "You always used to say that you would rather have married a Jewish man and lived a normal life. But when our day of destruction was upon us, then I knew that God himself had placed you in the palace. What seemed like bad luck to us was really part of God's plan."

Once again Esther simply nodded. She loved seeing her cousin so excited, and his idea was exciting to her as well. "Do you have a name for the holiday?"

Mordecai lifted the parchment for Esther

to see for herself. "It shall be called Purim[1], to remind us that even when things seem to happen by chance, we are still within God's control. Our God is truly a great God!"

---

[1] Jewish people everywhere still celebrate Purim, the Feast of Lots, usually in mid-March.

YOUNG READER'S CHRISTIAN LIBRARY

Be sure to check out other books in this series!

Written just for readers ages 8 to 12, these stories really come to life with dozens of illustrations. Kids will learn about the people, events, and ideas that had a tremendous impact on Christian history.

Paperback, 192 pages each

ONLY $1.49 EACH!